WELCOME! We hope you enjoy this Fave Art-12 album collection of favorite paintings (classic & modern). Most are copied from the internet, posters, prints and books. You may display this book as coffee table book in your living room, as conversation piece. You may give this as gift. You may cut out and frame each page. Each work is 8.5x11 inches and suitable for framing, and for wall decors.

Mother & Child by Joeyboi Galang, 2016

The ISBN Code Numbers of this book are:
ISBN-13: 978- 1547228133 & ISBN-10: 154722813X
Printed in USA. Free to copy by anybody. Why copy? Just buy the book.
Book List at - http://tinyurl.com/mj76ccq & http://www.jobelizes6.wix.com/mysite.
My contact email is job_elizes@yahoo.com. (Tatay Jobo Elizes, Pub.)

Juan Luna's "Bulaquena", 1890s – courtesy of Edgard O. Cruz at facebook

Juan Luna's Portrait of a Lady, 1890s – courtesy of Edgar O. Cruz at facebook

Unknown Pinoy beautiful abstract painting discovered online

WELCOME! We hope you enjoy this Fave Art-12 album collection of favorite paintings (classic & modern). Most are copied from the internet, posters, prints and books. You may display this book as coffee table book in your living room, as conversation piece. You may give this as gift. You may cut out and frame each page. Each work is 8.5x11 inches and suitable for framing, and for wall decors.

2000-year tree in South Africa, called The Tree of Life, Boabab tree.
Hollowed out trunks provide shelters to 40 people, provide 4500 liters
of water, bark fibers used as rope, fresh leaves are medicinal.
(this is a picture, not a painting, worth displaying)

Maria Clara portrait by Juan Luna, 1890s, gift to Jose Rizal for his Noli Me Tangere, courtesy of Phils My Phils at facebook

Modern Manila Girl, in oil, by Fernando Amorsolo, used as cover in Phil. Magazines, 1928-29 – courtesy of Edgar O. Cruz, facebook

Bisaya Girl, water color by I.L.Miranda, circa 1928-29, used in cover Of Phil. Magazine – courtesy of Edgar O. Cruz, facebook

Ilocano Girl, pastel, by I.L. Miranda, circa 1928-29, used as cover in Phil. Magazine. – courtesy of Edgar O. Cruz, facebook

Tagalog Girl, pastel, by Pablo Amorsolo, circa 1928-29, used as cover in Phil. Magazine. – courtesy of Edgar O. Cruz, facebook

Bicolana Girl, pastel, by Pablo Amorsolo, circa 1928-29, used as cover In Phil. Magazine. – courtesy of Edgar O. Cruz, facebook

Igorot Girl, pastel, by Pablo Amorsolo, circa 1928-29, used as cover In Phil. Magazine. – courtesy of Edgar O. Cruz, facebook

Mandaya Girl, water color, by I.L. Miranda, circa 1928-29, used as cover In Phil. Magazine. – courtesy of Edgar O. Cruz, facebook

Igorot Girl, pastel, by Pablo Amorsolo, circa 1928-29, used as cover In Phil. Magazine. – courtesy of Edgar O. Cruz, facebook

Igorot Girl, pastel, by Pablo Amorsolo, circa 1928-29, used as cover In Phil. Magazine. – courtesy of Edgar O. Cruz, facebook

Filipina Girl, in oil, by Fernando Amorsolo, used as cover in Phil. Magazines, 1928-29 – courtesy of Edgar O. Cruz, faceboo

Igorot Girl, pastel, by Pablo Amorsolo, circa 1928-29, used as cover in Phil. Magazine. – courtesy of Edgar O. Cruz, facebook

Igorot Girl, pastel, by Pablo Amorsolo, circa 1928-29, used as cover In Phil. Magazine. – courtesy of Edgar O. Cruz, facebook

Rural scene, artist unknown

Spread of Christianity, artist unknown

Abstract painting, artist unknown

Abstract painting, artist unknown

Grace before meals by Vicente Manansala, 1970s

Magbabayo, pounding rice, by Vicente Manansala, 1970s

WELCOME! We hope you enjoy this Fave Art-12 album collection of favorite paintings (classic and modern). Most are copied from the internet, posters, prints and books. You may display this book as coffee table book in your living room, as conversation piece. You may give this as gift. You may cut out and frame each page. Each work is 8.5x11 inches and suitable for framing, and for wall decors.

Candle Vendors, by Vicente Manansala, 1970s

Catching Fish by Anita Magsaysay-Ho, 1970s

By Manuel Rodriguez, age 99 in 2017, foremost Philippine Printmaker

By Cesar Legaspi, another famous Pinoy Painter, 1980s

By Jackson Pollock, 1949, Untitled, Green Silver (priceless)

By Gustav Klimt, 1903, Birch Tree (famous)

WELCOME! We hope you enjoy this Fave Art-12 album collection of favorite paintings (classic & modern). Most are copied from the internet, posters, prints and books. You may display this book as coffee table book in your living room, as conversation piece. You may give this as gift. You may cut out and frame each page. Each work is 8.5x11 inches and suitable for framing, and for wall decors.

Lubay. Modernitistic, by Candelaria (Pinoy painter)

Mag-ina sa Banig, 1960, by Nestor Leynes (classic)

By Isaia, Deviant Art, Disney Filipino Folktale

Fish Vendor, Artist Unknown

Family Relaxing, artist unknown

Mother & Child, by Marticio

Bibingca or Rica Cake, Artist unknown

Fruit Vendor, modernistic, Artist unknown

Itik (Ducks), by Pepe de Jesus (classic)

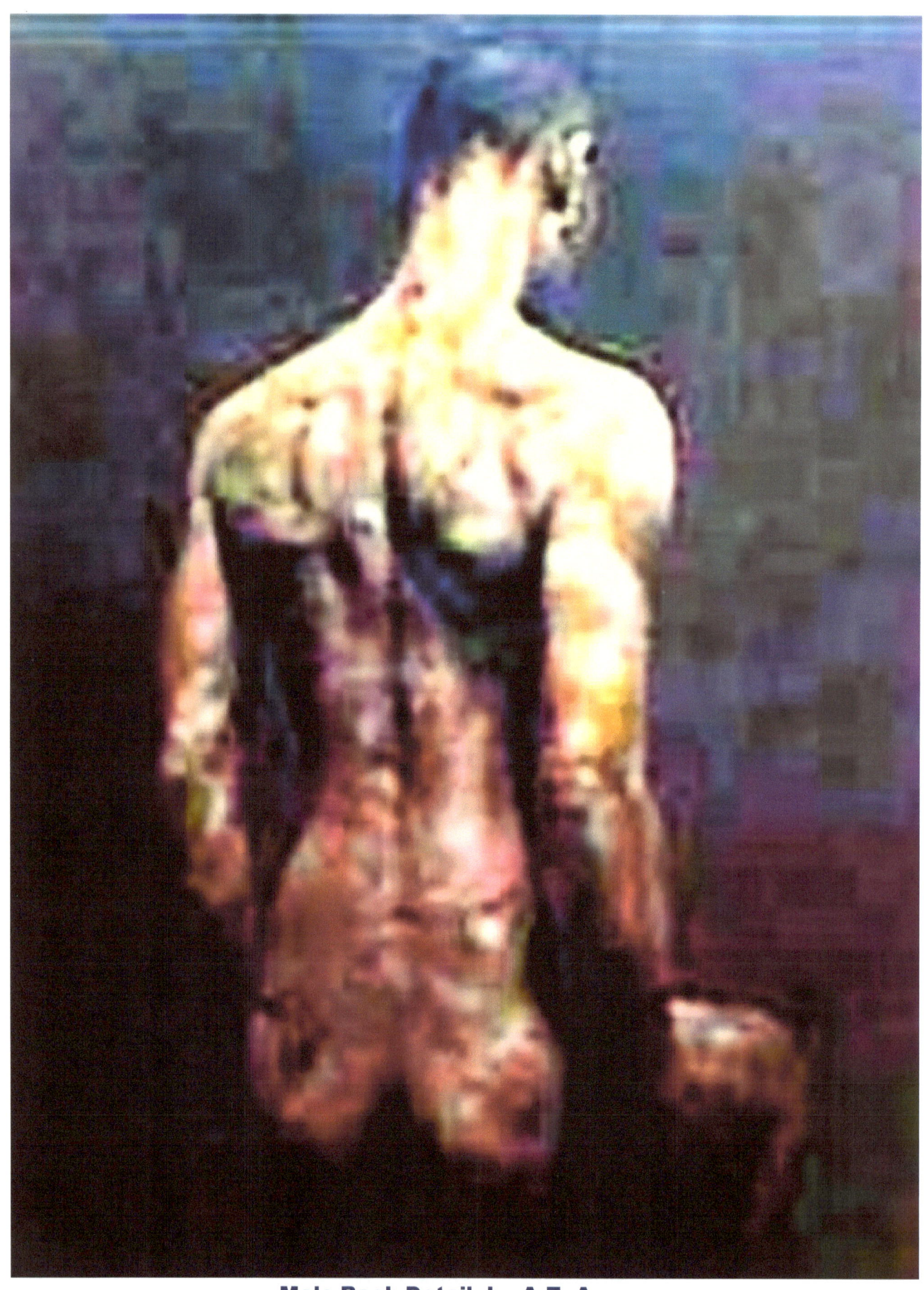

Male Back Detail, by A.Z. Anwar

www.ingramcontent.com/pod-product-compliance
Lightning Source LLC
Chambersburg PA
CBHW051108180526
45172CB00002B/824